Born to be Wild

Little Guinea Pigs

Anne Royer

Words that appear in the glossary are printed in **boldface** type the first time they occur in the t

GARETH**STEVENS**
PUBLISHING
A Member of the WRC Media Family of Companies

A Growing Family

Guinea pig babies are called puppies. If you look closely at a female guinea pig when she is almost ready to give birth, you can see the puppies moving underneath the fur on her stomach. Guinea pig puppies are born very quickly. Depending on the number of babies, a whole **litter** of puppies is born in only ten to thirty minutes. The newborn puppies are wrapped inside a thin tissue that the mother guinea pig must lick off.

A little guinea pig snuggles close to its mother after it is born.

What do you think?

How long do female guinea pigs carry their babies before giving birth?

a) about twenty weeks

b) about three weeks

c) about ten weeks

Female guinea pigs carry their babies for about ten weeks before giving birth.

The fewer the puppies, the longer a female guinea pig carries them inside her body. If, for example, a female guinea pig is carrying only two puppies, they will stay inside her body for almost eleven weeks. If she is expecting four, five, or six puppies, she will carry them for about nine weeks. By the time a mother guinea pig is ready to give birth, she grows to almost twice her normal weight.

Mother guinea pigs usually have three or four babies in a litter. Some, however, might have litters of seven or eight puppies.

At birth, guinea pig puppies already have hair covering their bodies, and they can move on their own. They also have claws and permanent teeth, and they can see.

A mother guinea pig can feed only two babies at a time, so the puppies need to take turns. They will drink their mother's milk for three weeks.

5

Teeth That Keep Growing and Growing

When guinea pigs are three weeks old, they weigh about 7 ounces (200 grams). They are big enough now to feed themselves. Guinea pigs are **vegetarians**. They eat only plants, such as fruits and vegetables, and dried food made especially for guinea pigs. Their long front teeth, called **incisors**, never stop growing. The animals must constantly gnaw, or chew, on things to wear the incisors down and keep them from becoming too long. A guinea pig's incisors are as sharp as razor blades. The animal uses them to bite into and cut food. It uses its back teeth to chew the food.

What do you think?

What does a guinea pig do when its food is dirty?

a) It refuses to eat the food.

b) It buries the food.

c) It washes the food.

Guinea pigs eat vegetables, including carrots, spinach, celery, cucumbers, lettuce, and green peas. They also eat dry hay and green plants such as dandelions and grass.

Guinea pigs are very picky about their food. They will refuse to eat food that is dirty, so the food should be placed in a clean bowl and should not sit out too long. Although guinea pigs eat grass, it is a hard food for them to **digest**. Both guinea pigs and rabbits digest grass in an unusual way. When they first eat the grass, it is not digested completely. The undigested grass comes out of their bodies in soft pellets, or droppings. Guinea pigs eat these droppings to digest the grass further.

When a guinea pig's incisors grow too long, the animal will **salivate**, or drool, a lot. Long teeth might also injure the guinea pig's mouth. A **veterinarian**, or animal doctor, can shorten the teeth by grinding them down.

Guinea pigs drink a lot of water. Because they are as careful about drinking clean water as they are about eating clean food, their water needs to be changed every day.

8

Guinea pigs are fully grown by the age of eight months.
A puppy gains about 0.2 ounces (5 g) every day.

A guinea pig does
not sleep all night.
It often wakes up for
a nighttime snack.
After nibbling on a
carrot or chewing on
some lettuce, it falls
asleep again.

An Affectionate Pet

Guinea pigs are popular pets. A pet guinea pig often cuddles against its owner or even gives little kisses. It is a very friendly **rodent**. It does not usually bite and is not in a bad mood very often, but before a guinea pig gets to know its owner, it can be shy. Taming a guinea pig takes time. It needs to learn how its owner smells and the sound of its owner's voice before it can become a good pet. Then, it will purr like a cat, let its owner scratch its head, and might even do somersaults on its owner's lap.

In the wild, guinea pigs live in groups of about ten animals. A **domesticated,** or tamed, guinea pig also enjoys being in a group.

What do you think?

Why do a guinea pig's teeth sometimes chatter, or click against each other?

a) The guinea pig is cold.

b) The guinea pig is angry.

c) The guinea pig is hungry.

When a guinea pig acts strangely or makes a sound like a scream, it is just trying to communicate. It peeps, like the whistle of a teakettle, when it wants food. When it growls, it is scared. When it lies on its back without moving, it is trying to protect itself by pretending to be dead. A guinea pig's teeth chatter when it is angry, and if the animal stretches its head forward, be careful! It is about to bite! When guinea pigs make clucking sounds, however, they are just trying to tell you they are happy.

A guinea pig becomes unhappy when it lives alone. If a guinea pig is taken away from its group too suddenly, it might starve itself to death.

Although a guinea pig loves being with others, it also enjoys being in a quiet place of its own sometimes, to take a nap or to play hide-and-seek.

A group of guinea pigs usually has only one male. If a group has more than one male that is able to **reproduce,** the males may fight with each other.

Growing Up Fast

At only four weeks old, a female guinea pig can already **mate** and have babies of her own. A mother guinea pig and her babies will be healthier, however, if the female mates for the first time when she is between three and seven months old. If a female guinea pig does not mate until after she is seven months old, she may have trouble giving birth. As adults, female guinea pigs are called sows, and males are called boars — just like the pigs on farms.

What do you think?

How many litters of puppies can a female guinea pig have each year?

a) one

b) five

c) three

A male guinea pig is able to mate when he is only three weeks old, but he will be healthier if he does not mate until he is at least five months old. The **dominant** male in a group mates with all of the females.

A female guinea pig can have up to five litters of puppies each year.

After a female guinea pig gives birth, she needs to be separated from the males of the group. If she mates right after having a litter of babies, she will have another litter. Because a female guinea pig can have four or five litters in a year, she may have to take care of as many as twenty to twenty-five pups! A mother guinea pig should be left alone with her pups for at least one month so that she can take proper care of them. In the wild, female guinea pigs usually have fewer babies. A wild guinea pig typically has only one litter of pups each year.

Until guinea pig puppies are about three weeks old, they are not very active. After that, they will spend their days running and somersaulting.

Mother guinea pigs seem content to live alone with their pups, without the father guinea pigs around. Mothers living in a group all take care of their babies together.

Who Are You?

No one knows for sure how these small, furry animals came to be called guinea pigs, but people have many different ideas. Are they cousins of the big pigs that live on farms? Of course not! But, just like farm pigs, guinea pigs have stocky, rounded bodies. Guinea pigs also oink, squeal, and snort. Guinea pigs originally came from South America. Some people think the name is a misspelling of Guiana, an area in South America. Others think that the animals were brought to Europe on ships that stopped in the African country of Guinea. Another idea is that a guinea pig could be bought for a British coin called a guinea.

Wild guinea pigs live in small groups. For shelter, they dig burrows, or settle in empty burrows that were made by other small animals, or they make nests in holes between rocks. They are most active at sunset, when they are out looking for food.

What do you think?

What other kind of animal is also called a "guinea pig"?

a) a hamster

b) a lab animal

c) a field mouse

Besides being very popular pets in North America, guinea pigs are also used a lot by scientists as lab animals. Their name, in fact, has come to mean any animal or person being used for testing or experiments. In France, a guinea pig is called an Indian pig. This name is based on the fact that these animals originally came from Latin America, which early explorers thought was India.

A silkie guinea pig has shiny hair that can grow up to almost 12 inches (30 centimeters) long. A silkie's beautiful, long hair must be brushed every day.

The American guinea pig is also known as the English guinea pig. It has short, smooth fur that can be white, cream, black, brown, beige, gold, red, lilac, or two or more of these colors.

One of a guinea pig's largest cousins is the Patagonian hare, or mara. This South American animal weighs 15 to 20 pounds (7 to 9 kilograms). It looks a lot like a big rabbit, and it has long legs, so it can run very fast.

Some guinea pigs have hair that is ruffled and grows in a circular swirl around a center, like flower petals. These swirls of hair are called rosettes.

21

Guinea pigs are **mammals**. They are also rodents. Like all rodents, they have two pairs of incisors that never stop growing, and they must gnaw to keep their teeth from becoming too long. Wild guinea pigs live in groups on the grassy plains of South America. They use holes in rocks or burrows as shelters. Wild guinea pigs live about four years. Tamed guinea pigs live about eight years.

There are at least fourteen kinds of wild guinea pigs. They are related to porcupines and **chinchillas**.

The whiskers on a guinea pig's face help it detect **obstacles** so it can move around in the dark. A guinea pig's whiskers should never be cut or pulled out.

Guinea pigs have four toes on their front feet and three toes on their back feet. All of their toes have claws on them.

An adult guinea pig is about 8 to 14 inches (20 to 36 cm) long. Adult guinea pigs weigh between 1 and 3 pounds (450 and 1,360 g).

Even though they have small ears, guinea pigs can hear very well. They can hear high sounds that people cannot hear and can tell the footsteps of different people apart.

Guinea pigs' coats can be smooth or ruffled. The coats can be one solid color or have bands or patches of two or more colors.

Unlike many other rodents, such as beavers, squirrels, and mice, guinea pigs do not have long tails.

When a guinea pig does not get enough exercise, its claws grow too long. They can be trimmed with a small pair of clippers.

GLOSSARY

chinchillas — small, squirrel-like animals with soft, gray fur

digest — to break down food into a form that can be absorbed and used by the body

domesticated — tamed, not wild

dominant — having the most power or control

incisors — sharp front teeth that animals use for cutting food

litter — a group of young animals born at the same time to the same mother

mammals — warm-blooded animals that have backbones, give birth to live babies, feed their young milk from the mother's body, and have skin that is usually covered with hair or fur

mate — (v) to join together to produce young

obstacles — objects that block forward movement or make movement difficult in some way

reproduce — to have babies or offspring

rodent — an animal with large incisors, such as a rat or a beaver

salivate — to make a lot of liquid, or saliva, in the mouth

vegetarians — people and other animals that do not eat meat

veterinarian — a doctor who is trained to take care of sick or injured animals

Please visit our web site at: **www.garethstevens.com**
For a free color catalog describing Gareth Stevens Publishing's list of high-quality books and multimedia programs, call 1-800-542-2595 (USA) or 1-800-387-3178 (Canada). Gareth Stevens Publishing's fax: (414) 332-3567.

Library of Congress Cataloging-in-Publication Data

Royer, Anne.
   [Cochon d'Inde. English]
   Little guinea pigs / Anne Royer. — North American ed.
      p. cm. — (Born to be wild)
   ISBN 0-8368-6166-3 (lib. bdg.)
   1. Guinea pigs—Juvenile literature. I. Title. II. Series.
QL737.R634R6813   2006
636.935'92—dc22   2005051730

This North American edition first published in 2006 by
Gareth Stevens Publishing
A Member of the WRC Media Family of Companies
330 West Olive Street, Suite 100
Milwaukee, Wisconsin 53212 USA

This U.S. edition copyright © 2006 by Gareth Stevens, Inc.
Original edition copyright © 2002 by Mango Jeunesse.

First published in 2002 as *Le cochon d'Inde* by Mango Jeunesse, an imprint of Editions Mango, Paris, France. Additional end matter copyright © 2006 by Gareth Stevens, Inc.

Picture Credits (t=top, b=bottom, l=left, r=right)
Bios: C. Testu 5(t); M. Gunther 8(br); D. Halleux: 5(b), 22. Cogis: Lanceau cover, back cover, title page, 22–23; Français 6, 12, 14; Alexis 15; Labat 17; Rocher/Labat 21(tr). Colibri: J. L. Paumard 2; A. Labat 9(t); C. Testu 7, 9(b), 21(b); S. Breal 13(b); F. & J. L. Ziegler 10, 21(tl). Jacana: J. L. Dubois 8(tl). Sunset: R. Maier 4; Bringard 13(t); Horizon Vision 16; G. Lacz 18, 20.

English translation: Muriel Castille
Gareth Stevens editor: Barbara Kiely Miller
Gareth Stevens art direction: Tammy West
Gareth Stevens designer: Jenni Gaylord

Printed in the United States of America
1 2 3 4 5 6 7 8 9 10 09 08 07 06